America's Unhealthy Lifestyle:
Supersize It!

Obesity: Modern-Day Epidemic

America's Unhealthy Lifestyle:
Supersize It!

by
Ellyn Sanna

Mason Crest Publishers
Philadelphia

First printing
1 2 3 4 5 6 7 8 9 10

Library of Congress Cataloging-in-Publication Data

Sanna, Ellyn, 1958–
   America's unhealthy lifestyle : supersize it! / by Ellyn Sanna.
      p. cm. — (Obesity : modern-day epidemic)
   Includes index.
   ISBN 1-59084-942-6—ISBN 1-59084-941-8 (series)
   1. Obesity—United States—Juvenile literature. 2. Nutrition—United
States—Juvenile literature. 3. Food habits—United States—History—
Juvenile literature. 4. Food industry and trade—Health aspects—United
States—Juvenile literature. 5. Convenience foods—Health aspects—
United States—Juvenile literature. 6. Lifestyles—Health aspects—United
States—Juvenile literature. I. Title. II. Obesity (Philadelphia, Pa.)
   RA645.O23S26 2005
   616.3'98'00973—dc22
                                        2004028650

Produced by Harding House Publishing Service, Inc., Vestal, New York.
Cover design by Michelle Bouch.
Interior design by Michelle Bouch and MK Bassett-Harvey.
Printed in the Hashemite Kingdom of Jordan.

Contents

Introduction

We as a society often reserve our harshest criticism for those conditions we understand the least. Such is the case with obesity. Obesity is a chronic and often-fatal disease that accounts for 400,000 deaths each year. It is second only to smoking as a cause of premature death in the United States. People suffering from obesity need understanding, support, and medical assistance. Yet what they often receive is scorn.

Today, children are the fastest growing segment of the obese population in the United States. This constitutes a public health crisis of enormous proportions. Living with childhood obesity affects self-esteem, employment, and attainment of higher education. But childhood obesity is much more than a social stigma. It has serious health consequences.

Childhood obesity increases the risk for poor health in adulthood and premature death. Depression, diabetes, asthma, gallstones, orthopedic diseases, and other obesity-related conditions are all on the rise in children. Recent estimates suggest that 30 to 50 percent of children born in 2000 will develop type 2 diabetes mellitus—a leading cause of preventable blindness, kidney failure, heart disease, stroke, and amputations. Obesity is undoubtedly the most pressing nutritional disorder among young people today.

This series is an excellent first step toward understanding the obesity crisis and profiling approaches for remedying it. If we are to reverse obesity's current trend, there must be family, community, and national objectives promoting healthy eating and exercise. As a nation, we must demand broad-based public-health initiatives to limit TV watching, curtail junk food advertising toward children, and promote physical activity. More than rhetoric, these need to be our rallying cry. Anything short of this will eventually fail, and within our lifetime obesity will become the leading cause of death in the United States if not in the world.

Victor F. Garcia, M.D.
Founder, Bariatric Surgery Center
Cincinnati Children's Hospital Medical Center
Professor of Pediatrics and Surgery
School of Medicine
University of Cincinnati

Chapter 1

The Supersized Lifestyle

Jennifer Scott isn't fat. Neither is Jared, her fifteen-year-old younger brother. And their little sister Caitlyn is a skinny little stick. So the Scotts don't worry much when they hear that America is in the midst of an obesity crisis. They eat whatever they want, and unlike many Americans, they don't worry about Calories, carbs, or fats.

Too Busy to Cook

Like many teens, the Scotts love fast food. What's more, with their family always on the go, fast food provides a handy solution for hurried suppers or meals on the road. Mr. Scott is a computer engineer; Mrs. Scott is a college professor; and neither parent gets home from work before 5:30 or 6:00 in the evening. Between Jared's sports, Jennifer's violin lessons and orchestra rehearsals, and Caitlyn's after-school art classes, most weeknights the family is dashing from place to place.

Even if Mr. or Mrs. Scott has a chance to make supper at home, chances are at least one member of the family won't have time to eat it; the Scotts usually end up making a fast swing through the drive-thru so no one's starving. On weekends, the Scotts make lots of trips to visit both sets of grandparents, who live out of town in opposite ends of the state. To save time, the

Almost two-thirds—64.5 percent—of all adult Americans are overweight or obese. That's about 127 million people.

family often eats on their way, usually at one of their favorite fast-food places. If they're really rushed, they just eat in the car and keep right on driving. Sometimes Mrs. Scott complains that they never eat "real food"—but she's just too busy to know what else to do.

The Scotts have a supersized lifestyle, one that's jam-packed with activities. They're busy, successful people, involved with the world around them. And that's good, right? So what if they don't have time to eat like folks did back in the fifties and sixties, in the days of *Leave It to Beaver* and *Father*

Calories: The Measurement of Food Energy

A Calorie is a thermal unit of energy; in other words, it's a way to measure the heat produced by a specific substance. Calorie with a capital "C" stands for large calorie or kilogram calorie. This is the type of Calorie used to measure the energy in food. One Calorie is equal to the amount of energy it would take to heat one kilogram of water (approximately one liter or four and a quarter cups) one degree Celsius. There is also a measurement known as a small calorie, or calorie with a lowercase "c." This type of calorie is used in chemistry, physics, and other disciplines that need to accurately measure tiny amounts of heat. A small calorie is the amount of heat it takes to heat one gram of water—one milliliter or about 20 drops from an eyedropper—one degree Celsius. A single food Calorie contains one thousand small calories.

Knows Best? Life is bigger and faster now. Fast food is just one of the many adaptations people have had to make in order to cope with the realities of modern life. At least that's what Mr. and Mrs. Scott tell themselves. And it's not so bad, after all. The food is fast and convenient—and it tastes good.

The Pleasures of Fast Food: Big Portions and Mouthwatering Taste

Two of the Scott teenagers also have plenty of opportunities to enjoy fast food for lunch. Their high school allows them to leave campus for lunch, so both Jared and Jennifer usually grab a soda or milk shake, burger, and fries at McDonald's or Burger King; the food there is a whole lot better than in the school cafeteria, and the portions are bigger. Jared is always hungry lately, so he usually gulps down a couple of Big Macs

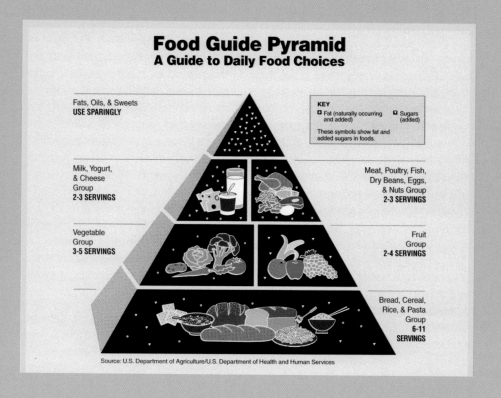

Food Guide Pyramid
A Guide to Daily Food Choices

Fats, Oils, & Sweets
USE SPARINGLY

KEY
◻ Fat (naturally occurring and added)   ◻ Sugars (added)
These symbols show fat and added sugars in foods.

Milk, Yogurt, & Cheese Group
2-3 SERVINGS

Meat, Poultry, Fish, Dry Beans, Eggs, & Nuts Group
2-3 SERVINGS

Vegetable Group
3-5 SERVINGS

Fruit Group
2-4 SERVINGS

Bread, Cereal, Rice, & Pasta Group
6-11 SERVINGS

Source: U.S. Department of Agriculture/U.S. Department of Health and Human Services

Jennifer's Typical Lunch

	A Meal at McDonald's			
Menu Item	Calories	Fat Grams	Protein Grams	Carbs Grams
Big Mac™	560	32.4	25.2	43
Fries, large	400	21.6	5.6	46
Shake, chocolate	320	1.7	11.6	66
TOTALS	1280	55.5	42.4	155

Source: McDonald's and USDA data bases

So what's wrong with this lunch? Well, it provides 1,280 Calories, which is more than half the Calories Jennifer needs each day. Given that she skips breakfast and doesn't always have time to eat much for supper, that's not so bad. The problem is that this meal's Calorie proportions are skewed toward fat. Take a look:

fat: 39 percent of daily requirement
protein: 13 percent of daily requirement
carbohydrates: 48 percent of daily requirement
(half from sugar)

This meal provides a satisfactory portion of protein, but 63 percent of its Calories come from fat and sugar. This wouldn't be so bad if Jennifer balanced her nutrition through the rest of the day's food. Unfortunately, however, the rest of her day's nutrition is not much different.

Why Does It Matter What We Eat?

The U.S. Department of Agriculture (USDA) and the U.S. Department of Health and Human Services (HHS) recommends that in order to stay healthy, teenage boys and active men should consume 2,800 Calories per day. Teen girls and active women should consume 2,200 Calories per day. These Calories should come primarily from carbohydrates in the form of breads, cereal, rice and pasta (six to eleven servings); vegetables (three to five servings); fruit (two to four servings); dairy (two to three servings); and nondairy proteins including lean meats, poultry, fish, dried beans, eggs, and nuts (two to three servings). Why? Because researchers have found that these proportions of food are what our bodies need in order to build and maintain their cells.

According to Eric Schlosser, author of Fast Food Nation, *the aroma of food can be responsible for as much as 90 percent of its flavor.*

> *Scientists believe that human beings acquired the senses of taste and smell in order to avoid being poisoned: in the natural world, things that taste and smell good are generally good for us, while things that are bitter or smell bad will often make us sick.*

or Whoppers, plus a large order of fries. Jennifer never has time for breakfast before the bus comes in the morning, so by lunchtime she's usually pretty hungry too.

The fast-food restaurants are also fun places to hang out with their friends. The restaurants are bright, cheerful, and modern. And just walking in the door makes Jared's and Jennifer's mouths water.

There's a good reason for this. The Scotts have probably never heard of the flavor industry—but it's responsible for the taste of most of the foods they eat. Through chemical additives, the flavor industry puts the vanilla taste in Jennifer's milk shake and that wonderful aroma in Jared's fries. The flavor industry is also the reason why a pizza tastes the same at the Scott's local Domino's as it does when they stop in for a Domino's pizza when they're on vacation on the other side of the country. Many of fast-food restaurants' highly processed foods would taste like textured water—or worse—without a hand from the flavor industry. (Flavor additives aren't only used in fast foods. They also keep the cake mix sitting in the Scotts' cupboard tasting the same for months.)

The Secret Ingredient

Unless your family buys only fresh homegrown foods that they prepare themselves, chances are most of the foods you eat have a secret ingredient: flavor enhancers. Today the flavor industry is a multi-billion dollar giant that produces chemical additives for almost every type of food on the market. Some flavors are considered natural, derived from naturally occurring substances such as cinnamon, coffee, or lemon. However, the largest class of flavor molecules used today is synthetics that have no counterpart in the natural world.

"Just about anything . . . that comes in a can, a jar or a box has artificial flavors in it," explained Glenn Roberts, executive director of the Flavor and Extract Manufacturers Association. The fragrance and flavor industry has grown 5.4 percent annually over the past five years, to an expected $18.4 billion in 2004—but the industry maintains a low profile. "Because we are suppliers to manufacturers of branded ingredients, we are not the entity that people are familiar with," Roberts said. In other words, fast-food companies like Burger King and Pizza Hut get the fame, while the flavor industry stays quietly in the background. Citing intellectual property concerns, the Food and Drug Administration does not require flavor companies to disclose the ingredients of their products. This means that consumers really don't know what makes their food taste so good.

Sit-Down Fast Food

The Scotts don't *always* eat at fast-food restaurants of course. At least once or twice a week, they have time for a nice sit-down meal at their favorite family restaurant. Although it's not the same as home cooking, Mr. and Mrs. Scott tell themselves it's the next best thing. The Scott teenagers like it better than at-home meals because they get to choose what they want. Even Caitlyn has at least one favorite meal on the menu.

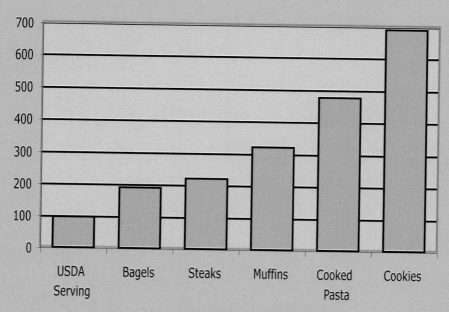

Portion Sizes for Common Foods
(% USDA Recommended Size)

Unfortunately, however, the behind-the-scenes action is much the same at many sit-down restaurants as it is at fast-food places. The Scotts' favorite restaurant chains (places like Friendly's, Olive Garden, TJIF, and Applebee's) copy the operating techniques of the fast-food chains. Although their menus are more varied, they still have standard menus for all restaurants in the chain. They serve the same burgers, french fries, and chicken sandwiches as the fast-food restaurants, plus other food items that can also be easily *mass-produced*.

In both fast-food and family restaurant chains, the food is produced in a central factory where it is portioned, frozen, and shipped to each restaurant of the chain. What's wrong with that? Well, the food that looks and smells so good is a long way from your mom's home cooking. A juicy-looking steak, for example, is often not solid meat. Instead, raw meat was shredded into flakes at a central factory; glues and extra fat were added; and the "steak" was pressed under a steamroller. (Particleboard is made pretty much the same way, only from wood fibers instead of meat.) The final touches are the marks added by a machine specially designed to create the impression that the "steak" was grilled on an open fire.

By the time a meal like this reaches the Scotts' table, the food has undergone many processes. It may have been frozen, thawed, and refrozen several times. Chemical additives were added to make sure the food didn't spoil along the way. Taste enhancers make up for flavor drained during manufacturing. And lots of salt was dumped in to mask any off-flavors that might remain. In the end, the sit-down meal has no more nutritional worth than what the Scotts get in their fast-food meals. The family restaurants cost a little more; the pace is more relaxed; and the atmosphere is a bit higher class—but the menu items are just as high in fat, salt, and chemical additives.

What's the Matter with Freezing Food?

Freezing breaks down a food's structure. For a meal to survive freezing and cold storage, the manufacturer adds chemicals. By the time the food reaches your plate, it offers no better nutritional value than a fast-food meal.

A bottle of Coca-Cola once contained an average 6.5 ounces; now it contains 20 ounces. Sixty-four-ounce sodas can pack a whopping 800 Calories. That means a child who needs 1,500 Calories a day could get more than half of them from just one drink.

Home-Cooked Fast Food

Caitlyn Scott is still in middle school, where leaving campus for lunch isn't an option. She brings a "healthy" lunch packed by her mom: a sandwich, carrot sticks, an apple, a bag of chips, a juice box, and some cookies. Caitlyn doesn't really like very many foods, though, so she usually just eats the chips, drinks the juice, takes a bite or two from the sandwich and the apple, and then finishes up with the cookies. Most days, she also buys an ice-cream sandwich. The rest goes in the trash can, and her mom is none the wiser.

Caitlyn is a picky eater, and she hates the nights when the family does eat at home. She doesn't like cooked vegetables; she doesn't like most meat (although she loves chicken nuggets); and she's not too fond of salad. Mrs. Scott worries because Caitlyn is so thin—but she feels better when she sees the way Caitlyn eats at breakfast, scarfing down a whole package of frozen waffles or most of a box of breakfast bars. After all, Mrs. Scott tells herself, the waffles and breakfast bars are fortified with vitamins. She doesn't stop to consider that these prepackaged foods are actually just another sort of fast food.

Fast food isn't just in restaurants; it's in grocery stores as well. Gone are the days of making everything from scratch. Today you can buy just about any food, from frozen french fries to salad to pasta dishes, already-prepared, prepackaged, precooked, and bagged, boxed, canned, dehydrated, or frozen. Like the foods served in both fast-food and many family restaurants, these meals have been frozen and refrozen; food enhancers and other chemicals have been added to them; and their nutritional values have been reduced. Most are high in fats and sugars and low in vitamins and other nutrients. But

Eating Wisely

Like the Scotts, the average American family eats more restaurant food than they buy in supermarkets. This means it's often hard for them to assess the nutritional value of what they're eating. The government has mandated nutrition labeling for supermarket products—but there's usually no nutrition guide when you order in a restaurant. However, some restaurant chains have Web sites where this information is available. Check out this Web site for a list of restaurants that offer this information: http://diabetes.about.com/cs/nutritiondiet/a/fast_food_guide.htm

they're fast, easy, and convenient—and that's important to busy families like the Scotts. For the Scotts and many other families, fast food has become a way of life.

Supersized Portions

The portion sizes the teenage Scotts encounter in fast-food restaurants are many times bigger than the portions their parents ate when they were teenagers. A study published by the *Journal of the American Medical Association* found that between the years of 1971 and 1999, portion sizes for certain foods increased dramatically. Of the foods studied—hamburgers, Mexican foods, soft drinks, snacks, and pizza— all but pizza increased. Hamburgers became, on average, more than a fifth larger. A plate of Mexican food was more than one-quarter larger. Soft drinks expanded by more than half their previous size, and salty snacks like potato chips, pretzels, and crackers grew by 60 percent. The most striking increases occurred in fast-food restaurants.

There's a financial reason for this. The *profit margins* for fast foods can be huge. *Agricultural subsidies*, mass production, low labor costs, and

In 1957, a typical fast-food hamburger weighed one ounce and had 210 Calories. Today the typical fast-food hamburger weighs six ounces and has 618 Calories.

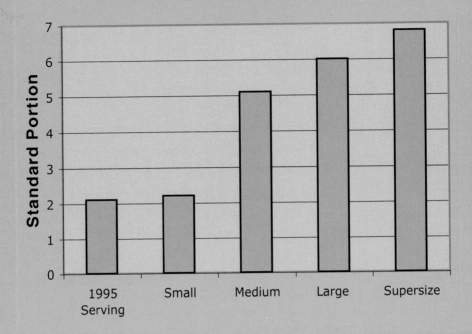

McDonald's Fries and Size Inflation

other cost-saving systems make fast food so plentiful and so cheap that companies don't gain anything by withholding it from customers. Some of these foods only cost the restaurants pennies, but they sell these foods for dollars.

For example, if a restaurant gives customers twice as many fries, it will only cost the company ten cents more. But if the company can get the

Obesity now surpasses smoking as the leading cause of premature and preventable deaths.

A Deadly Equation

Increasing portion sizes would be disturbing just on their own, but combined with another factor—decreasing activity—they are especially alarming. We Americans are not only eating more than ever before, we're also less active than we've ever been. The human body did not evolve to sit in a car, behind a desk, in front of a computer, or before a television. Yet for many of us, these are the activities that take up the majority of our time. For about 99 percent of human history (and for most humans in the world today) people never had to consciously think about exercising because their whole lives involved exercise. Foraging and hunting took huge amounts of energy. Farming is also Calorie-burning work. Even with the rise of the industrial age, when many people in the Western world left farming to make money in mines, factories, and industry-driven trades, most of the work was still just as physical. It's really only within the last fifty to sixty years that American lifestyles changed so dramatically.

> **A recent study found that 14 percent of all deaths are caused (directly or indirectly) by a combination of diet and physical inactivity.**

customer to pay thirty cents more for those extra fries, the company has just made twenty cents in profit. For fast-food restaurants, bigger portion sizes mean bigger profits.

Other restaurants have discovered this same economic secret. And portion increases aren't limited to restaurants, either. The same study found that these increases occurred in the American home as well. Whether eating out or eating in, Americans are eating more than ever before—and those extra Calories are a factor in America's escalating obesity crisis.

Sometimes, the Scott teenagers overhear their parents discussing the family's eating habits, making resolutions to eat healthier. The younger Scotts just roll their eyes and smile; they know their parents' resolutions will only last as long as the next school night when all five members of the family are dashing in opposite directions. What difference does it make, anyway? After all, they're not fat—and they like fast food.

> **Today's American children may be the first generation in modern history to have a shorter average lifespan than their parents.**

How Is Obesity Determined?

One tool doctors use to evaluate body size is body mass index (BMI). BMI is a mathematical formula that uses weight and height to determine whether someone's body is a healthy size. The formula is as follows:

[Weight in pounds ÷ (Height in inches x Height in inches)] x 703 = BMI

A BMI that is:
Below 18.5 = Underweight
18.5 – 24.9 = Normal
25.0 – 29.9 = Overweight
30.0 and Above = Obese

Example for a person who weighs 132 pounds and is five-feet, four-inches (64 inches) tall:
[132 pounds ÷ (64 inches x 64 inches)] x 703 = 22.66 (a normal weight)

BMI is not always an accurate measure of health. Muscle tissue is much denser and heavier than fat tissue. Since BMI only measures height and weight, an extremely muscular and fit person could have the same BMI as an unfit person who has a large amount of fat. For this reason, a better measure of overweight and obesity is body fat percentage—the amount of your body's tissue that is made of fat. Doctors, nutritionists, and fitness experts use tools to measure different areas of the body. These measurements yield one's body fat percentage.

FIND YOUR BMI

LOCATE YOUR HEIGHT HERE

LOCATE YOUR WEIGHT HERE

BMI (kg/m²)	19	20	21	22	23	24	25	26	27	28	29	30	35	40
Height	Weight (lb.)													
4' 10"	91	96	100	105	110	115	119	124	129	134	138	143	167	191
4' 11"	94	99	104	109	114	119	124	128	133	138	143	148	173	198
5' 0"	97	102	107	112	118	123	128	133	138	143	148	153	179	204
5' 1"	100	106	111	116	122	127	132	137	143	148	153	158	185	211
5' 2"	104	109	115	120	126	131	136	142	147	153	158	164	191	218
5' 3"	107	113	118	124	130	135	141	146	152	158	163	169	197	225
5' 4"	110	116	122	128	134	140	145	151	157	163	169	174	204	232
5' 5"	114	120	126	132	138	144	150	156	162	168	174	180	210	240
5' 6"	118	124	130	136	142	148	155	161	167	173	179	186	216	247
5' 7"	121	127	134	140	146	153	159	166	172	178	185	191	223	255
5' 8"	125	131	138	144	151	158	164	171	177	184	190	197	230	262
5' 9"	128	135	142	149	155	162	169	176	182	189	196	203	236	270
5' 10"	132	139	146	153	160	167	174	181	188	195	202	207	243	278
5' 11"	136	143	150	157	165	172	179	186	193	200	208	215	250	286
6' 0"	140	147	154	162	169	177	184	191	199	206	213	221	258	294
6' 1"	144	151	159	166	174	182	189	197	204	212	219	227	265	302
6' 2"	148	155	163	171	179	186	194	202	210	218	225	233	272	311
6' 3"	152	160	168	176	184	192	200	208	216	224	232	240	279	319
6' 4"	156	164	172	180	189	197	205	213	221	230	238	246	287	328

Source: USDA

But even though all three of the Scotts are well within the "normal" range for weight, each of them is participating in supersized America's lifestyle, a lifestyle that has led to a health crisis. Well over half the U.S. population is either overweight or obese, a fact that contributes to serious health risks. Today none of the Scotts teenagers are obese or even overweight—but if they don't change their eating habits, as the years go by, they too, like many other Americans, are likely to find themselves accumulating extra pounds.

Fast food's supersized portions are an *intrinsic* aspect of the modern U.S. lifestyle. Fast food is wed to both Americans' hurried, hectic lifestyles and their appetites. What's more, it's a natural outgrowth of America's history.

Chapter 2

The History of American Eating

Americans weren't always fat. In fact, it's a fairly recent phenomenon. Until the twentieth century, most people simply worked too hard to be overweight. Maybe a few very wealthy people consumed more Calories than they used—but most Americans were hardworking farmers. And yet the roots of today's obesity crisis can be found in America's past.

A Legacy of Pride and Plenty

Long ago, the first Americans, the Natives of the *Western Hemisphere*, lived in harmony with nature. They regarded the Earth as their mother, an *entity* to be respected, cared for, and intimately loved. The Earth gave them everything they needed, including sustenance for life. Food was a sacred gift from Mother Earth, and they often referred to the plants and animals they used for food as sisters and brothers. Their diets were regulated by the Earth's cycles, and times of feasting were followed by lean times. Few if any of these earliest Native Americans were overweight.

But life in North America changed with the coming of the Europeans. These white-skinned people brought new ways of doing things, and Native wisdom and traditions were overpowered in the onslaught of the new population. Colonial Americans looked at food far differently than the Natives. While the Indians saw the Earth's fruits as honored and well-loved family members, white farmers regarded nature as a dangerous adversary, an opponent to be defeated with cunning and strength.

At first, the early settlers struggled to find ways to survive on the continent they called the "New World." The land was wild, and the climate was often far different from what they were accustomed to back in Europe. These long-ago pioneers in a new land were courageous and hardy, however, willing to endure danger and hardship in order to build new homes. They cleared the land and built fertile farms. Eventually, they became prosperous.

Blame Evolution!

If you're like many people, you might have a sweet tooth, love salty foods, and crave fatty and Calorie-rich foods. In fact, fat, salt, and sugar, the things we should eat the least, are often the things we crave the most. But why would your body desire foods you don't need?

Michael D. Lemonick, senior science writer at *Time* magazine, reported in a 2004 article that human beings evolved to crave high-Calorie foods like those containing fats and sugars. Life was hard for early humans. Early humans probably spent nearly every moment of every day searching, chasing after, and fighting for their food. And more food wasn't guaranteed to show up tomorrow. If you had it, you'd better eat it now, as much of it as you could get! Those who ate the most Calories survived, and those who ate the least, well . . . they died. It's only within the last century (and in the wealthiest countries) that food has suddenly become so plentiful and easy for most people to obtain. Our evolution, however, occurred over millions of years in which our bodies told us to eat every Calorie-rich food in sight. It's not easy to give up millions of years of craving—so most people still find the fattiest, saltiest, and most sugary foods to be the tastiest and most desirable. And the bigger the serving, the better it looks!

For America's European settlers, the New World was a land of promise and plenty. As the years went by, more and more **immigrants** crossed the Atlantic to escape the poverty and hunger of the "Old World," seeking America's opportunities for freedom, wealth, and security. The lands along North America's East Coast filled up with people, and settlers began to look West, seeking new farmland and new opportunities. America was a big land, full of unlimited possibilities. These concepts of bigness and plenty became important aspects of how Americans viewed themselves.

The United States as a young nation was full of optimism and a heady sense of its own strength. After all, hadn't America beaten the British Empire, the strongest nation of its day? As a free and independent nation, America's abundant and fertile lands allowed its people to raise quantities of corn, which in turn fed countless cattle. The people of the United States were no longer poor and hungry as many of them had once been. Instead, Americans' hope and pride were fed by hearty meals of beef and potatoes, chicken and dumplings, ham and biscuits. These plentiful foods nourished and symbolized Americans' self-confident spirit. What's more, agriculture—the production of food—made America a rich and powerful nation, able to take its place at the head of the class. Americans had conquered their land, and now they would control the world as well.

New Means to Wealth and Abundance

Beginning in the late nineteenth century, food began to be mass-produced, mass-marketed, and standard-ized. Factories processed, preserved, canned, and packaged a wide variety of foods. Processed cereals, which were originally promoted as one of the first health foods, quickly became a regular feature of the American breakfast. During the 1920s, a new industrial technique—freezing—emerged, and businesses took advantage of all the new opportunities presented by Clarence Birdseye's "Quick Freeze Machine." Increasingly, processed and nationally distributed foods domi-nated the nation's diet—and food processing became an important American road to wealth.

Many of the ideas that would create fast food, however, did not originate in the food industry at all. Instead, they were born from the car industry. In the early twentieth century, Henry Ford believed he could make cars in a more efficient and cost-effective way. To do so, he imagined the automobile as a conglomerate of different components or parts. These parts were mass-produced to be identical and interchangeable (for example, the engine in one car was identical to the engine in every other car and could therefore be put in any car). The work of putting an automobile together was likewise broken down into all its different components, and one person was assigned to each task. This eliminated the need for expensive skilled labor, because workers no longer needed to know how to build a car; they just needed to know how to perform one task, like tightening a specific bolt or putting on a tire. To save time, Ford put the cars on an assembly line. Now workers never even

wasted time walking around. The cars just rolled to the workers; the workers performed their specific tasks; and off the cars went down the line. The result was amazing: a huge increase in production, a dramatic decrease in production costs, and a steady supply of cars that average Americans could afford. Within twenty years, well over fifteen million automobiles had been sold in the United States, and American society had changed forever. Now the world looked even bigger to Americans. The future was a place of wide-open possibilities.

In 1948, Richard and Maurice McDonald applied Henry Ford's principle for building cars to making food. In what they called their "Speedee Service System," the McDonald brothers removed from their menu any food that needed silverware (this left the basics like hamburgers, fries, and milk shakes), standardized the menu (all the hamburgers would be cooked and served exactly the same way, and customers could not get substitutions), and divided the food preparation into small jobs with each task being performed by one person. The McDonald brothers no longer needed skilled cooks; they just needed people who could put burgers on a grill, drop fries into hot oil, or run a milk shake machine. If workers needed fewer skills and less training, then they could also be paid less money. Furthermore, by doing away with plates and silverware and by wrapping all the food in paper or other disposable products, the McDonalds eliminated the need for dishwashers and the cost of dishes and equipment, another labor-reducing, money-saving move. With their new system the McDonalds could make food faster and cheaper than anyone else, allowing them to undercut competitors' prices and still make enough profit to get rich. Fast food was born.

Today we are so accustomed to prepared, prepackaged fast foods, that the McDonalds' system doesn't seem revolutionary. In fact, you might think it's the only logical way for a restaurant to run. How else would a restaurant get its food made and delivered to its customers in a quick, affordable manner? That's exactly the point: before the McDonald brothers introduced this system, food preparation was time consuming and expensive. Restaurants simply weren't affordable for families to eat at on a regular basis. If you were a single person, you might be able to save your pennies for a night out with friends, but if you were a family with children, dinner at a restaurant would be a rare and special event. With cheaper fast food, however, a family could now afford to go out to dinner.

Soon customers were lining up around the block for a McDonald's hamburger, and restaurant owners and *entrepreneurs* from around the country were traveling to see the McDonald's Speedee Service System with their own eyes. After witnessing the food-production miracle, they began opening fast-food restaurants of their own, each trying to improve on the others' ideas. Fast-food restaurant owners realized that the key to fast food was preparation and *mechanization*. The more the foods could be prepared ahead of time, the quicker they could be served up when ordered—and the more specialized machines businesses could invent, the less they needed to rely on people to cook the food. Soon machines that cooked two sides of a burger at once, mixed numerous milk shakes at a time, or performed other amazing tasks were simplifying the work, eliminating the need for numerous employees, reducing wages, and reducing the cost of the final product.

The Wave of the Future

A few years after the McDonald brothers introduced their Speedee Service System, a man named Ray Kroc paid them a visit. Mr. Kroc was the salesman who sold the milk shake machines McDonald's used. He couldn't understand why any restaurant needed six milk shake machines, each capable of making five shakes at a time. When Kroc saw the line outside of McDonald's, however, he suddenly understood this was an altogether different operation than any he had seen before.

Ray Kroc didn't have much education—he had dropped out of high school and never attended college—but he had a real gift for sales. Soon he was giving Richard and Maurice the sales pitch of his life. If they sold him the right to open McDonald's *franchises*, Kroc said, he would make them rich. Richard and Maurice, however, were already rich. Their one little restaurant was bringing money in hand over fist, and they didn't really care to work any harder. Now they preferred to enjoy life and the prosperity it brought. But when it came to making a sale, Ray Kroc was the best. He assured the McDonald brothers there wouldn't be any additional work for them. All they had to do was sit back and watch the money roll in.

McDonald's serves 46 million people every day around the world. In 1996, the McDonald's company opened a new restaurant somewhere every three hours.

Although Richard and Maurice McDonald introduced the Speedee Service System, Ray Kroc made McDonald's what it is today. Kroc realized that America was fundamentally different from the country it had been just a few decades ago. It was the age of the automobile. Gone were the days of being born, living, and dying in the same town. Americans were now mobile, and as highways stretched across the country, people were enjoying their new freedom. Ray Kroc dreamed that, no matter where Americans traveled, there would be a McDonald's on the horizon. Kroc suspected that people arriving in an unfamiliar town would be more likely to go to a McDonald's, where they knew exactly what would be on the menu, than to the local mom-and-pop restaurant they knew nothing about. Kroc believed the key to McDonald's success would be *uniformity*. No matter who opened a McDonald's franchise or where in America it was located, it would guarantee the same menu and service as every other McDonald's in America.

Soon McDonald's restaurants were opening all over the country. Menu items were added and operating systems were perfected.

Dunkin' Donuts sells 6.4 million donuts per day. That's enough to circle the earth twice.

With the company's huge growth, however, uniformity became both more important and more difficult to achieve. How could Kroc ensure that a hamburger served in a California McDonald's tasted exactly the same as a hamburger served across the country in a New York McDonald's? If the food was going to be identical, it had to all come from the same place and be prepared in exactly the same way. Huge off-site facilities capable of mass-producing enough McDonald's food to supply hundreds of restaurants nationwide rose. Now McDonald's food was prepared, prepackaged, and in many cases precooked before it even entered the restaurant's kitchen. It was then preserved and shipped to all corners of America. This food preservation was key to the success of the McDonald's system, and it wouldn't have been possible without the incredible advances in technology being made at the time. New methods of freezing, packaging, dehydrating, and other forms of food preservation ensured food didn't spoil before arriving at a McDonald's kitchen.

For years, other fast-food chains copied what McDonald's did, and its practices became the standards by which the entire fast-food industry was run. Today it seems like there's a fast-food restaurant on every corner of every town. McDonald's, Burger King, KFC, Wendy's, Taco Bell, Pizza Hut, Subway, Arby's, Hardee's, Roy Rogers, Dairy Queen, Dunkin' Donuts, Krispy Kreme, A&W, Domino's Pizza, and countless more compete for Americans' appetites. Then there are the semi-fast-food restaurants: Olive Garden, Red Lobster, Long John Silver's, Friendly's, Denny's, Ruby Tuesday, Applebee's, Pizzaria Uno, Cracker Barrel, Chili's, LongHorn Steakhouse, Hard Rock Café—all restaurants that combine fast-food principles (like precooked, prepackaged foods) with a sit-down restaurant atmosphere. What's more, fast food isn't just in restaurants; as we discussed in chapter 1, it's in grocery stores as well. Gone are the days of making everything from scratch. Americans' relationship with food has changed forever.

Destined to Overeat?

But the wave of the future swells out of the past. The attitudes of early Americans toward food still shape our minds today. Even religion plays its role.

Americans don't like boundaries. When colonial Americans wanted to spread into the West, they ignored the claim Native tribes had to those lands; instead, America's leaders came up with the notion of Manifest Destiny, the idea that it was God's plan for Americans to inhabit the continent from Atlantic to Pacific. Modern Americans seem to be applying a new kind of Manifest Destiny to the world of food and portion size; where religion once spoke out against the sin of *gluttony*, today, even the most conservative of American Christians see little wrong with overeating.

Unlike much of the world's populations, Americans often feel they are entitled to plentiful food. Our ancestors worked hard to achieve America's prosperity, and we take for granted our right to revel in America's abundance. In most of our minds, bigger is always better.

Chapter 3

A Passion for Bigness

- Eating with Our Eyes

- Americans' Love Affair with Bigness

- The Supersized Body

- A Supersized World

Eating with Our Eyes

"Your eyes are bigger than your stomach."

At one time or another, all of us have heard the familiar warning against overeating. We don't usually listen. Instead, we judge our portion sizes by what looks good to us, rather than by the actual healthy capacity of our stomachs.

According to Leon Rappoport, author of *How We Eat: Appetite, Culture, and the Psychology of Food*, "Americans eat with their eyes, but the French eat with their noses." In other words, the French emphasize the *quality* of the eating experience; they savor the aroma of each bite—but Americans care more about *quantity*. They judge food by how it looks, and most important, by its size.

Tiny wild strawberries, for example, are actually far sweeter than the enormous hothouse strawberries sold in supermarkets—but Americans don't care. They want strawberries the size of small apples. A small home-made muffin may be more flavorful and certainly healthier than the giant muffins offered at supermarkets and donut shops—but Americans want the BIG muffin.

And once we have that humongous muffin, we eat the entire thing—every sweet, fat-laden morsel. In fact, the more we're served, the more we eat.

Recent research has found that Americans truly do judge their food with their eyes rather than any other faculty (including their common sense). The larger the portion, the more Calories people consume. "Portion size has been

suggested to be one of the major culprits in the obesity epidemic," said Barbara Rolls, a nutrition researcher and professor of *biobehavioral* health at Penn State University.

In Rolls' study (published in the March 2004 edition of *Obesity Research*), she and her team served the study participants an average portion of a baked pasta dish, along with one that was 50 percent larger. The entrées were served in the same-sized dish but on different days, so both would appear the same and diners would have no basis for comparing them. When served

The first McDonald's hamburgers were 1.6 ounces; that size is still available, but the Big Mac and Quarter Pounder each weigh around 4 ounces.

2001 Press Release from Jack in the Box Restaurants: Meaty Magnitude

Big burgers rule at Jack in the Box restaurants, now home to perhaps the meatiest and cheesiest burger in the fast-food industry—the Triple Ultimate Cheeseburger.

Consisting of three beef patties, two slices of American cheese, one slice of Swiss cheese, mayo-onion sauce, and a jumbo bun, the Triple Ultimate Cheeseburgers is a two-fisted burger sure to satisfy the heartiest of appetites.

"The Triple Ultimate Cheeseburger is definitely not for the faint of heart," said Tammy Bailey, senior product manager for Jack in the Box. . . .

Though this is Jack's first triple-decker, it's not the chain's first behemoth burger. Over its fifty-year history, the chain has introduced such heavyweights as the Bacon Ultimate Cheeseburger and the Ultimate Cheeseburger, but none have matched the meaty magnitude of the Triple Ultimate Cheeseburger.

the regular entrée, people ate an average 399 calories worth of pasta; when served the larger portion, they consumed an average 571 calories. What's more, when eating the larger portion, diners also ate more side dishes, racking up an extra 159 calories on average. Surprisingly, their stomachs did not accommodate the larger entrée by eating less of everything else, or even by eating less during another meal. Instead, they simply absorbed the extra calories.

Another experiment by Rolls (reported in March 2004 by Jon Bonné of MSNBC) showed that people served chips several hours before dinner consumed more total calories when they ate a larger bag of chips; they didn't compensate for their pre-dinner snack by eating less at the meal.

Americans' Love Affair with Bigness

You can tell a lot about how Americans think about food by the words that show up on menus. Apparently, Americans' appetites are piqued by words like "mega," "monster," "extreme," "whopper," "ultimate," "king," and "biggie." You never find words like "modest," "just enough," "delicate," or "dainty." We want our foods to be as big as the great outdoors. And we hate to have limits imposed on our appetites.

The Biggest Nation

Americans like big things. After all, we live in one of the biggest nations in the world when it comes to geographical area—and the biggest when it comes to political power. It's no wonder then that we love tall skyscrapers and super malls. We shop in mega-supermarkets and we drive enormous SUVs. We live in multi-bedroom, multi-bathroom houses, and our vacation "cottages" look like mansions. (Meanwhile, Europeans are driving tiny Minis or Smart Cars that are barely bigger than an American motorcycle; and even the wealthy often live in modest houses with only a single bathroom.)

That's probably why all-you-can-eat buffets are so popular with Americans. So are all-you-can-eat fish fries and pancake breakfasts. When it comes to food, Americans love to get their money's worth.

The fast-food movement may have capitalized in new ways on Americans' fondness for big meals—but the American passion for bigness is nothing new. In *Revolution at the Table: The Transformation of the American Diet*, Harvey Levenstein reports:

> To nineteenth-century observers, the major difference between the American and British diets could be summed up in one word: abundance. Virtually every foreign visitor who wrote about American eating habits expressed amazement, shock, and even disgust at the quantities of food consumed. . . .
>
> . . . the apparent indifference of American hotel patrons to wasting food struck Europeans as a product of its abundance in America. "The thing which strikes me most disagreeably . . . is the sight of the tremendous waste of food that goes on at every meal," wrote a European recalling his sojourns in nineteenth-century American hotels.

The Supersized Body

Limitless abundance, bounty without restriction: those have been the hallmarks of the American mind-set toward food. In the nineteenth century, Americans' concept of the ideal body corresponded to their preferred level of food intake. The principal causes of death and disability among Americans in the mid-1800s were infectious diseases linked partly to poor or inadequate food intake—so the goals of health officials and the food industry were the same: encourage people to eat more of all kinds of foods. In fact,

physicians instructed the public to *gain* weight. Full, curvy bodies became **synonymous** with health and wealth; stoutness in both men and women was a symbol of prosperity, a sign one could afford to eat well. Skinny, bony bodies were a sign of poverty and malnutrition. Plump, round, **Victorian** figures were in, and heavy was "sexy." A good layer of abdominal and hip fat was thought to mean a woman was more fertile, able to successfully endure childbirth, and better equipped to fight off infectious disease—all desirable traits. Men considered chubby arms and cheeks beautiful, and gaunt hollow looks were "low class."

If Americans tended to weigh in on the "plump" side, however, the majority of the population fell short of obese. Health issues related to weight were not such problems when Americans were expending most of their calories through one form of hard physical labor or another. As the workforce became more **sedentary**, however, it's no wonder that many Americans now struggle with the issue of obesity.

Americans don't want to be fat. On any given day, according to recent surveys published in the *Journal of the American Medical Association*, 115 million adult Americans are dieting for one reason or another. That's 55 percent of the total population, and these figures don't even include teens. Author

From 1960 to 2002, the average weight jumped from 166.3 pounds to 191 pounds for men and 140.2 pounds to 164.3 pounds for women. The average weight of a ten-year-old has also increased about 11 pounds in the last 40 years.

Frances M. Berg cites a recent study of New York high school girls, which revealed that 70 percent of high school females had tried to diet at least once. The diet industry is a booming business—but few Americans manage to successfully lose weight and keep off the pounds on a long-term basis.

Americans are conflicted. They don't want to be overweight; in fact, they'd rather be model-thin. But at the same time, they love to eat. Diet

No Appetite for Smaller Servings

The growing publicity around the supersizing trend has many Americans pointing fingers at fast-food restaurants for their role in the current obesity crisis. Unfortunately, businesses that try to serve up healthier, smaller servings have found that Americans don't buy enough of their food to keep them in business. "Consumers will tell you they're concerned about their health," market researcher Bob Sandelman reports in the January 2005 issue of *Fortune Small Business* magazine, "but most really just go for convenience and taste."

The History of American Fast Food

Apparently, Americans have always had a tendency to eat and run, a trait that the fast-food industry appealed to rather than created. One nineteenth-century European wrote:

> For the American man, meal time is not . . . a period of relaxation, in which his mind seeks repose in the bosom of his friends; it is only a disagreeable interruption of business, an interruption to which he yields because it cannot be avoided, but which he abridges as much as possible.

Another European stated that the Americans' national motto was, "Gobble, gulp, and go."

plans that speak to these *paradoxical* feelings are particularly popular. A person on a low-carb, high-protein diet plan, for example, has to limit his intake of breads and pastas—but he can eat as much meat and fats as he wants. He may not be able to have his cake and eat it too—but he can certainly have his Quarter Pounder with Cheese and eat it too, so long as he doesn't eat the bun. In other words, he can still supersize it!

This year, Americans will digest approximately $2.4 billion worth of prepackaged weight-loss meals like Lean Cuisine® and NutriSystem®, $1.7 billion in shakes like Slim-Fast® and snack bars like Zone®, and then wash it all down with $15 billion worth of diet soda. That doesn't even begin to count all the books, magazines, club memberships, "miracle" drugs, and other products Americans will purchase. And yet, on average, they're still getting fatter.

Unfortunately, the long-term success rates of these diet plans are questionable. The bottom line seems to be that if Americans don't find new ways to think about themselves and food, the trend toward steadily increasing weight will continue. Many doctors see this trend as a health crisis as serious as cancer or AIDS. But not all Americans are willing to accept this perspective.

Like any health condition, obesity says nothing about the value of the individual; people who are overweight or obese are as intelligent, talented, and loveable as anyone else. Our culture is full of messages that say the opposite, and these voices need to be drowned out by the clear words of education and tolerance.

However, some people want to go a step further and say that being obese or overweight is an acceptable option, even a matter of personal choice. According to this perspective, if people keep getting bigger, then the world should keep pace with them.

Bigger Blue Jeans

In the 1960s and '70s, blue jeans were tight—skin tight. By the middle of the 1980s, the baby boomers who had been buying blue jeans in previous decades were still buying jeans—except now, these same individuals couldn't fit into the pencil-thin jeans of their youth. So Levi Strauss and Gap took a look at their sizing. Over night, what was once a "regular" cut was now a "slim." Jean buyers could suddenly pick from four new options: regular fit, easy fit, loose fit, and baggy fit. The new "fits" were simply bigger sizes without the bigger numbers.

A Supersized World

If you happen to be one of the millions of Americans who are obese, you are likely to encounter uncomfortable situations where your body just doesn't fit in the space provided. Booths in restaurants may be a tight squeeze, for instance, and so may airplane seats . . . turnstiles in subways . . . some car models . . . movie theater seats . . . even hospital beds.

But as America's obesity rate climbs to epidemic levels, many businesses have hit on a solution: they're supersizing the world to handle the overload. Some theaters now have seats that can convert two seats into one. Tiny steering wheels can be installed in some cars to allow more belly room. Ambulance companies are using "heavy-duty" models for certain patients; hospitals offer supersized rooms with special mattresses, bigger commodes, larger walkers, plus-sized hospital gowns, and "big-boy" wheelchairs. Even clothing sizes have been expanded to accommodate larger bodies; in many stores, yesterday's size 12 is today's size 8. Fashionable larger-sized clothing is also far more readily available than it was twenty or even ten years ago, and fashion consultants are careful to use words like "statuesque" and "voluptuous," rather than "heavy" or "overweight." Children's clothing industries are also accommodating kids' expanding waistlines by making roomier clothing to accommodate plus-size youngsters.

A Company Designed for Supersized Individuals

"Amplestuff is a unique company which was established in 1988 to serve the special needs of the millions of men and women who are plus or supersize. Some of our products are plus-sized versions of items that are readily available to average size people—such as our fanny packs, socks, or hospital gowns. Other products—such as airline seatbelt extenders and size-positive books and videos—are designed especially to solve the unique problems of larger people. We believe that no matter what your size, you deserve the best possible life right now. In fact, our company motto is 'Make your world fit you!'"

(from www.amplestuff home page)

But the question is: Do these innovations make the world a better place by allowing people of all shapes and sizes to feel more comfortable? Or do they simply make it easier for people to stay big by removing the constraints that were once signals that they needed to lose weight?

The line between *stigma* and healthy limits is a fine one. On the one hand, as a culture, we want to be accepting and tolerant of people, no matter their shape, color, gender, or abilities. On the other hand, obesity is not the

Obesity Trends Among U.S. Adults
1991
(BMI >30, or ~30 Lbs overweight for 5′ 4″)

No Data   <10%   10%-14%   15%-19%

One in twenty Americans is "morbidly obese"—more than 100 pounds overweight.

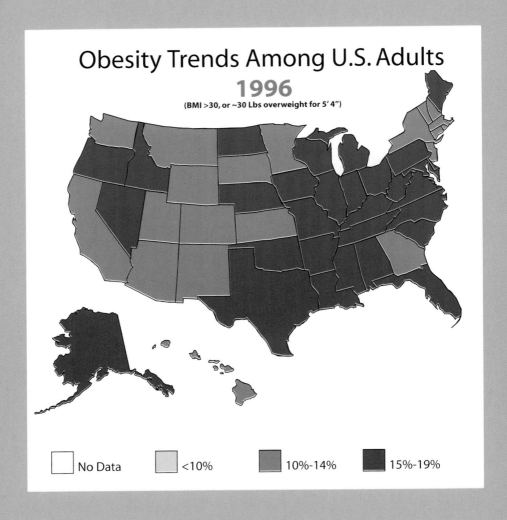

Obesity Trends Among U.S. Adults

1996

(BMI >30, or ~30 Lbs overweight for 5' 4")

| | No Data | | <10% | | 10%-14% | | 15%-19% |

same as some of the other differences that characterize human beings—and we're doing no one any favors (including ourselves) if we deny or obscure the very real health risks posed by obesity.

Obesity is a complicated and sensitive issue. Like the Scotts, the family we described in chapter 1, many of us are unwilling to examine our own participation in a supersized world. We all have blind spots, especially when it

Obesity Trends Among U.S. Adults
2001
(BMI >30, or ~30 Lbs overweight for 5′ 4″)

No Data   <10%   10%-14%   15%-19%   20%-24%   >25%

comes to our eating habits, and our mental landscapes are shaped by culture and history.

But these are not the only influences on our attitudes toward food. One of the most powerful forces in our supersized world is motivated only by profit. More and more, big business plays a role in the way we shape our world.

Chapter 4

Supersized Businesses

- Supersize Me
- The Power of Advertising
- Big Business and Children
- Big Business and Schools

The fast-food industry, the flavor industry, and the advertising industry are some of the biggest and most profitable businesses in the United States. Many Americans believe that these multi-million-dollar businesses play supersized roles in America's obesity crisis. But can big business really be blamed for the way Americans eat? After all, isn't personal responsibility a factor here? When confronted with the tempting aromas of a Big Mac and french fries, can't we "just say no"?

Supersize Me

A man named Morgan Spurlock doesn't think it's that simple. To prove his point, he conducted a supersized experiment. He decided to eat nothing but McDonald's food for thirty days.

Three doctors—a *general practitioner*, a *gastroenterologist*, and a *cardiologist*—a nutritionist, and a fitness expert tracked Spurlock's diet journey. At the beginning, they took blood tests, performed physicals, and reported he was in perfect health. Then Spurlock set rules for himself: he would only eat food sold at McDonald's; he would eat three meals every day; he would eat everything on the menu at least once; and if asked if he wanted his meal "supersized," he would say yes.

By the end of the month, Spurlock was in rough shape. He had gained twenty-four pounds, lost muscle strength, fallen into depression, had a huge surge in cholesterol, and his blood tests revealed his liver was close to failure. His doctors were concerned for more than his health; they were concerned for his life, and they called an end to the experiment. Spurlock immediately ditched McDonald's, began an exercise routine, embarked on a *vegan* diet, and worked for fourteen months to undo the damage done in just thirty days.

He also made a movie: *Supersize Me*. The film has achieved widespread acclaim and widespread criticism. The majority of that criticism comes directly from the fast-food industry.

McDonald's and other fast-food restaurants say Spurlock's choice to eat nothing but McDonald's food was completely irresponsible and grossly out of proportion with the average American's consumption of fast food. Fast-food industry leaders claim everyone knows that eating fast food all the time is bad for you and that, since nutrition information for their food is widely available, there is no excuse for individuals claiming they have been misled about the content of these foods. At the same time, industry representatives insist that most fast-food restaurants now offer healthy food options and that there is no reason why fast food can't be part of a healthy diet.

Spurlock counters that the corporations need to accept responsibility for their role in America's obesity crisis. "If you're McDonald's and you serve 46 million people a day," he says,

"and you tell me you have no obligation to educate your consumers and help them make the right choices. . . . That's absolute malarkey."

The Power of Advertising

Fast-food restaurants are businesses, and a business's goal is to make money—as much money as possible. Fast-food restaurants, therefore, are never going to encourage consumers not to eat their food! If they did, and if Americans listened, these enormous businesses would no longer be so enormous.

The fast-food giants are all in competition with each other for Americans' business. They don't want "responsible" fast-food consumers who only eat their unhealthy food on rare occasions. Instead, they want Americans to eat lots of their food and to eat it often. To encourage Americans to do this, businesses employ a powerful tool: advertising.

Big business has enormous advertising budgets—and those cheery commercials we see and hear so often are powerful and ever-present influences on our thoughts. If you hear something often enough, you start to believe it's true. And most of us are convinced that we "deserve a break today," or that we really need to "have it our way." If adults are susceptible to the simple magic of repetition and a catchy tune, think how much more vulnerable children are to advertising.

In the movie *Supersize Me*, Spurlock showed preschool children pictures of Jesus and Ronald McDonald. None of them knew who Jesus was—but all of them knew who Ronald McDonald was. Spurlock's point? Do parents really want MacDonald's advertising to play a larger role in their children's lives than the teachings of a religious leader like Jesus Christ?

Big Business and Children

Fast-food companies have realized something important when it comes to selling food: children usually have more influence with their parents than companies have. If a fast-food company can get children to want a product, those children will go to their parents, beg and plead, and often be successful in gaining what they want. When an advertisement aimed at an adult is successful, it may bring in one customer—but when an advertisement aimed at a child is successful, it often brings in three or more customers (the child as well as the child's parents and siblings).

Companies that advertised to children learned another important lesson: a child who is sold on a particular product is apt to be a customer for life. Companies believed that if they could get a child to become loyal to their brand and products, that child would remain loyal for the rest of her life. A

According to several recent studies, American children are exposed to 40,000 advertisements per year, most for fast foods and sugary or high-fat snacks. The research concludes that allowing children to watch television excessively is contributing to America's obesity problem.

child who started eating McDonald's before she tasted Burger King, the theory went, would continue eating McDonald's. A child who started drinking Coke before he tasted Pepsi would always prefer Coke. A person who had pleasant memories of slurping milk shakes as a child would slurp milk shakes as an adult.

Like so many other fast-food trends, McDonald's was the leader in the industry's advertising to children. Ronald McDonald, Hamburgler, and other characters appeared frequently during children's television programming. McDonaldlands and Playlands promised safe and wholesome fun for children, and Happy Meals complete with toys promised . . . what else? Happiness for kids.

McDonald's may have led the trend, but everyone else quickly caught on. The messages became more varied. Soon advertisements aimed at adults portrayed parents bringing their kids to a fast-food restaurant as a demonstration of good parenting, a way to make up for spending so much time at work away from the family, as well as a way to increase children's love and affection. Advertisements to children stressed the benefits for their parents—the food would be tasty, fast, and affordable—thereby arming the kids with nag-ammunition. The advertisements basically coached kids on what to say to convince their parents that going out for fast food was a good idea.

These forms of advertising are by no means limited to the fast food sold in restaurants. They are used to sell the packaged foods in vending machines and grocery stores as well. According to Marion Nestle of New York University's Department of Nutrition and Food Studies, about half of all advertisements directed toward children are for food. Ms. Nestle estimates that the food and drink industries spend $13 billion each year in advertising to kids.

Today, all kinds of people are employed in the business of marketing to children, and they use numerous tools to figure out how. Psychiatrists give analyses of children's dreams. Researchers explore the effects of bright colors on the child brain. Artists and designers develop eye-catching logos and child-friendly characters.

Young children are largely powerless against this onslaught. Studies have shown that young children can't distinguish between regular television entertainment and commercials. They don't know advertising is seducing their minds or that people with huge amounts of money and expertise are manipulating their emotions. They also don't have the skills to determine if advertising claims are trustworthy or not. If you tell a young child that a candy bar will make her strong, for example, she will believe you. Children are defenseless against advertising, and fast-food corporations know it.

A preschooler's risk of obesity increases by six percent for every hour of television she watches. If she has a television in her room, her risk of obesity increases by 31 percent.

Young children, however, aren't the only ones being targeted by advertising. In the last twenty years, teens have emerged as the focus for marketing dollars. Teens today have more *disposable income* than they have ever had before; each year, teens spend more than $150 billion from their own pockets. That's a huge amount of money, and fast-food companies want to get their share. To make sure they are getting as much of young people's money as possible, food and drink corporations have embarked on a huge and disturbing trend. They've moved into schools.

Big Business and Schools

Many American schools have faced serious financial difficulties in recent decades. Cuts in government spending, opposition to tax increases, and increasing enrollments have left some schools gasping for funds. When food and soft drink manufacturers began offering thousands of dollars for the privilege of getting their products and advertisements into the schools, many districts rushed to sign up.

Today, food and beverage companies not only have their vending machines in the hallways, advertisements on the walls, billboards on school buses, and logos plastered at sports events; they have also taken over many

A study of children who were six to eight years old found that 70 percent of them believed fast food was healthier than home-cooked food.

Once Again, Bigger Isn't Better

The big businesses that shape our appetites through advertising also shape other aspects of our world, including the environment. The huge quantities of beef and potatoes sold at fast-food restaurants are grown on enormous farms that are run like factories. Proponents of industrial agriculture claim that bigger is better when it comes to food production. They argue that the larger the farm, the more efficient it is.

But these huge corporate farms also mean the loss of family farms and rural communities. They destroy the natural environment in many regions of the world, including the fragile and precious rain forests of South America.

And is bigger really better? Numerous reports have found that smaller farms are actually more efficient than larger "industrial" farms. A study by the U.S. National Research Council concluded that "well-managed alternative farming systems nearly always use less synthetic chemical pesticides, fertilizers, and antibiotics per unit of production." Reduced use of these chemicals lowers production costs and lessens farms' harmful effects on the environment.

When we eat fast food, we need to remember that these processed and brightly packaged foods came from the Earth—and we need to know who paid the price. Ultimately, it will be ourselves.

> *In 1998, 89 percent of all children younger than eight years old visited McDonald's at least once a month.*

school lunch programs. America's government-sponsored school lunch program was never completely healthy to begin with, but today it has definitely taken a turn for the worse. For many schools, gone are the days of a sloppy joe, mashed potatoes, an apple, and a carton of milk. Today's children and teens go to the school cafeteria to grab pizza, cheeseburgers, chips, Coke, Pepsi, and fries. Depending on their contracts, schools may even get a percentage of the fast-food or beverage sales. Worse yet, some schools have contracts that *stipulate* minimum sales *quotas*; if those quotas aren't met, the school can lose some of the promised *revenues*. This has led to some schools allowing soft drinks and snacks to be purchased in the hallways and consumed in the classrooms. The need for money to support their programs has turned these schools into accomplices of the food and beverage industries.

In the end, however, none of us can entirely blame big businesses for our participation in a supersized culture. The truth is: as difficult as it may be, we do have the power to choose.

Faster Food from Supersized Businesses

For fast-food restaurants, time equals money. In fact, for every six seconds saved at the drive-thru, McDonald's researchers have found that sales are increased by 1 percent. That's a lot of money when your total sales are around $9 billion.

A robotics scientist named Kieran Fitzpatrick has come up with an idea that he says will cut waiting time at the drive-thru by two-thirds. He calls his idea HyperActive Bob—a camera on fast-food restaurants' roofs that tracks cars as they approach the drive-thru lane. Software within "Bob" then analyzes the cars' sizes and predicts how much food the passengers will order, allowing fast-food workers to be prepared ahead of the orders. (For example, the passengers in a mini-van will probably order more food than the passengers in a small sports car—and they're more apt to order burgers than chicken.) The system is already being used at fast-food restaurants in Pittsburgh, and other locations across the country are also interested in checking out HyperActive Bob.

Chapter 5

Where Do We Go from Here?

- A Different Mind-Set

- A Call to Action

- Making Your Own Choices

A Different Mind-Set

"The first step is a different mind-set," says Eugenia Calle, director of analytic *epidemiology* for the American Cancer Society. "We have to begin to equate normal weight with a state of health. . . . People will need to demand a world that makes it easier to stay at an appropriate weight. We want decent stairwells so that we can take the stairs at work. We don't want just vending machines full of crap. We have to change our cultural norms if we're going to get a hold of this."

Nationwide trends are reversed one individual at a time—and making wise daily choices can change an individual's life. These choices can be as simple as choosing to walk to the store instead of drive or take the bus . . . drinking water instead of soda . . . or stopping at a grocery store for fresh fruit

The trend toward supersizing shows signs of reversal. After years of complaints from nutritionists and consumer groups, McDonald's announced it was ending its supersized meal offers, and it has recently introduced new salads and fresh foods. Other fast-food restaurants are following their example.

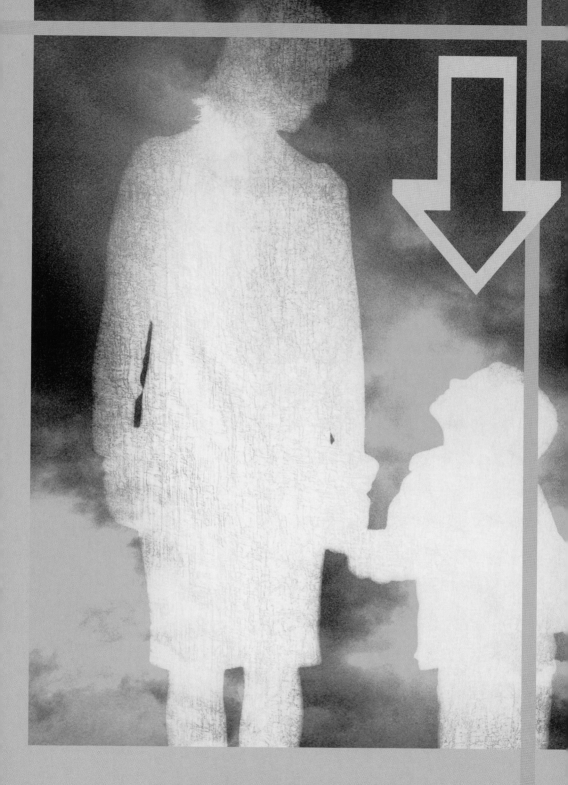

Pepsi has begun marketing an eight-ounce can, and Coke has long had eight-ounce servings, though they have been infrequently marketed. Still, many shoppers habitually look for the "deal"—which means they probably won't leap at the chance to buy smaller sizes until the larger ones are no longer available. It's hard to shell out 90 cents for a small can of soda when a twenty-ounce bottle for $1.50 is right next to it.

instead of grabbing a mammoth burger at a fast-food restaurant. They may be as difficult as turning off the television and finding new ways to occupy our time—or as easy as going for a walk with a friend. They may mean taking the time to think and be conscious about the way we are living our lives. In all likelihood, they will mean we have to take a long, hard look at some of our cultural assumptions. And there's no way around it; all these choices will require effort and determination.

A Call to Action

Recently, in what is called the Surgeon General's Call to Action to Prevent and Decrease Overweight and Obesity, HHS listed fifteen points of action as national priorities for everyone from individuals, to schools, to the government:

1. Change the perception of overweight and obesity at all ages. The primary concern should be one of health and not appearance.

2. Educate all expectant parents about the many benefits of breastfeeding. Breastfed infants may be less likely to become overweight as they grow older, and mothers who breast-feed may return to pre-pregnancy weight more quickly.

3. Educate health-care providers and health profession students in the prevention and treatment of overweight and obesity across the life span.

4. Provide culturally appropriate education in schools and communities about healthy eating habits and regular physical activity, based on the Dietary Guidelines for Americans, for people of all ages. Emphasize the consumer's role in making wise food and physical activity choices.

Creating an Exercise-Friendly World

Communities are finding that something as simple as building sidewalks and bike trails can have an impact on the prevalence of obesity. Creating an environment that encourages people to get around town on foot and by bicycle can have a significant impact on fitness.

At the American Community Gardening Association Conference in Philadelphia, farmer Abu Talib stated: "I believe that he who controls your breadbasket controls your destiny. . . . We're not just raising food, we're raising people. Everything starts with food. Life. Everything."

5. Ensure daily, quality physical education in all school grades. Such education can develop the knowledge, attitudes, skills, behaviors, and confidence needed to be physically active for life.

6. Reduce time spent watching television and in other similar sedentary behaviors.

7. Build physical activity into regular routines and playtime for children and their families. Ensure that adults get at least thirty minutes of moderate physical activity on most days of the week. Children should aim for at least sixty minutes.

8. Create more opportunities for physical activity at work sites. Encourage all employers to make facilities and opportunities available for physical activity for all employees.

9. Make community facilities available and accessible for physical activity for all people, including the elderly.

10. Promote healthier food choices, including at least five servings of fruits and vegetables each day, and reasonable portion sizes at home, in schools, at work sites, and in communities.

11. Ensure that schools provide healthful foods and beverages on school campuses and at school events by: enforcing existing U.S. Department of Agriculture regulations that prohibit serving foods of minimal nutritional value during mealtimes in school food-service areas, including in vending machines; adopting policies specifying that all foods and beverages available at school contribute toward eating patterns that are consistent with the Dietary Guidelines for Americans; providing more food options that are low in fat, calories, and added sugars such as fruits, vegetables, whole grains, and low-fat or nonfat dairy foods; and reducing access to foods high in fat, calories, and added sugars and to excessive portion sizes.

12. Create mechanisms for appropriate reimbursement for the prevention and treatment of overweight and obesity.

13. Increase research on behavioral and environmental causes of overweight and obesity.

14. Increase research and evaluation on prevention and treatment interventions for overweight and obesity, and develop and disseminate best practice guidelines.

15. Increase research on disparities in the prevalence of overweight and obesity among racial and ethnic, gender, socio-economic, and age groups, and use this research to identify effective and culturally appropriate interventions.

Making Your Own Choices

Researchers stress how important it is for children to shape good dietary habits while they're young as these habits are likely to follow them for the rest of their lives. Obviously, this observation holds much truth—but there's another side to the story as well. If you've grown up on a diet of one sort of supersized fast food or another, that doesn't mean you're condemned to eat fast food the rest of your life. During your teen years you have the chance to begin making up your mind for yourself about many aspects of life, including the food you eat. And as the years go by, you'll have more and more control.

If you look at your parents' food habits, you'll probably notice they're not the same as your grandparents'. The demands and routines of daily life have changed a great deal since your grandparents' day, and your parents have made their own decisions about how to adapt mealtime to the realities of their lives. You'll have the opportunity to do the same.

As a young adult, you may want to demonstrate your uniqueness—and the food you choose to eat is an important way to define your identity. Check out various approaches to food. (Vegetarian, vegan, all-natural, organic, macrobiotic are just a few examples—or you might want to look into other cultures' foods, such as Asian or Mediterranean.) Decide what appeals to you. Think about what you eat. Be conscious of what you put in your mouth.

You have information about what's best for your long-term health that your parents probably didn't have when they were shaping their eating habits. Use that information. Decide who you want to be. Supersize your consciousness.

Glossary

agricultural subsidies: Money given by the government to farmers to help support them.

biobehavioral: Relating to the interaction between behavior and biological processes.

cardiologist: A doctor who specializes in the diagnosis and treatment of heart disorders and related conditions.

conservative: Reluctant to change; wanting to preserve the status quo.

disposable income: Money available after expenses have been paid.

entity: Being, existence.

entrepreneurs: People who assume the risks and responsibilities of running a business.

epidemiology: The scientific and medical study of the causes and methods of transmission of disease.

franchises: Businesses that carry another company's name and sells its products.

gastroenterologist: A doctor who studies the treatment of diseases of the stomach, intestines, and related organs.

general practitioner: A doctor who treats general medical problems.

gluttony: The act of eating and drinking to excess.

immigrants: People who have come to another country and have settled there.

intrinsic: Belonging to something as one of its basic and essential elements.

mass-produced: Manufactured in very large quantities, especially using mechanization and assembly-line methods.

mechanization: The process of changing a procedure so it is performed by machines rather than by human labor.

paradoxical: Conflicting, opposing.

profit margins: The amounts by which income exceeds expenses.

quotas: Fixed numbers that are necessary to achieve.

revenues: Business income.

sedentary: Involving much sitting and little movement.

stigma: Shame or disgrace attached to something deemed socially unacceptable.

stipulate: Specify something as a condition when making an agreement or offer.

synonymous: Meaning the same as, or almost the same as, another word.

uniformity: Having the quality of being the same as others.

vegan: A diet that does not include meat, dairy products, or eggs.

Victorian: Relating to the period of the reign of British Queen Victoria.

Western Hemisphere: The half of the Earth that is west of the prime meridian, including North and South America.

Further Reading

Brownell, Kelly D. *Food Fight: The Inside Story of the Food Industry, America's Obesity Crisis, and What We Can Do About It*. New York: McGraw-Hill, 2004.

Critser, Greg. *Fat Land*. New York: Houghton Mifflin, 2003.

Esherick, Joan. *Diet and Your Emotions: The Comfort Food Falsehood*. Philadelphia, Pa.: Mason Crest, 2005.

Ford, Jean. *Diseases and Disabilities Caused by Weight Problems: The Overloaded Body*. Philadelphia, Pa.: Mason Crest, 2005.

Levenstein, Harvey. *Paradox of Plenty: A Social History of Eating in Modern America*. Berkeley: University of California Press, 2003.

_____. *Revolution at the Table: The Transformation of the American Diet*. Berkeley: University of California Press, 2003.

Libal, Autumn. *Social Discrimination and Body Size: Too Big to Fit?* Philadelphia, Pa.: Mason Crest, 2005.

_____. *Fats, Sugar, and Empty Calories: The Fast Food Habit*. Philadelphia, Pa.: Mason Crest, 2005.

Nestle, Marion. *Food Politics*. Berkeley: University of California Press, 2002.

Rappoport, Leon. *How We Eat: Appetite, Culture, and the Psychology of Food*. Toronto, Ont.: ECW Press, 2003.

Schlosser, Eric. *Fast Food Nation: The Dark Side of the American Meal*. New York: HarperCollins, 2002.

For More Information

American Obesity Association
www.obesity.org

Food and Nutrition Information Center
www.nal.usda.gov/fnic

Harvard School of Public Health: Food Pyramids
www.hsph.harvard.edu/nutritionsource/pyramids.html

Mind on the Media
www.mindonthemedia.org

National Center for Chronic Disease Prevention and Health Promotion's
Information on Obesity
www.cdc.gov/nccdphp/dnpa/obesity/index.htm

Obesity Information from MedlinePlus
www.nlm.nih.gov/medlineplus/obesity.html

The Surgeon General's Call to Action to Prevent and Decrease Overweight and
Obesity
www.surgeongeneral.gov/topics/obesity/

Publisher's note:
The Web sites listed on this page were active at the time of publication. The
publisher is not responsible for Web sites that have changed their addresses or
discontinued operation since the date of publication. The publisher will review
and update the Web site list upon each reprint.

Index

Picture Credits

Artville: pp. 34, 44

Bananastock: pp. 11, 20, 29, 43, 55, 93

Benjamin Stewart: p. 66

Centers for Disease Control and Prevention: pp. 69, 70, 71

Clipart.com: pp. 40, 41, 42, 49, 61

Colonial Williamsburg Foundation: p. 38

Daniel Boone Homestead: p. 37

Hemera: pp. 15, 24, 47, 53, 57, 59, 74, 76, 79, 84, 88, 90, 96

MK Bassett-Harvey: pp. 8, 32, 50, 67 (bottom right), 72, 86

Photos.com: pp. 52, 65

Raw Graphics: pp. 41, 46, 64, 75, 77, 92, 95

U.S. Department of Agriculture: pp. 13, 14, 19, 31

Biographies

Ellyn Sanna is the author of many fiction and nonfiction books for both children and adults. Her works include several books on food and dieting, such as *Dieting in Real Life* from Barbour Publishing and *Food Folklore* by Mason Crest Publishers.

Dr. Victor F. Garcia is the co-director of the Comprehensive Weight Management Center at Cincinnati Children's Hospital Medical Center. He is a board member of Discover Health of Greater Cincinnati, a fellow of the American College of Surgeons, and a two-time winner of the Martin Luther King Humanitarian Award.